SCATTER SEEDS *of* KINDNESS

Inspirational poems and short stories about life, love, and the things that shape our souls...

K.A. BLOCH

Copyright © 2022 K.A. Bloch.

All rights reserved. No part of this book may be used or reproduced by any means, graphic, electronic, or mechanical, including photocopying, recording, taping or by any information storage retrieval system without the written permission of the author except in the case of brief quotations embodied in critical articles and reviews.

This book is a work of non-fiction. Unless otherwise noted, the author and the publisher make no explicit guarantees as to the accuracy of the information contained in this book and in some cases, names of people and places have been altered to protect their privacy.

Because of the dynamic nature of the Internet, any web addresses or links contained in this book may have changed since publication and may no longer be valid. The views expressed in this work are solely those of the author and do not necessarily reflect the views of the publisher, and the publisher hereby disclaims any responsibility for them.

The author of this book does not dispense medical advice or prescribe the use of any technique as a form of treatment for physical, emotional, or medical problems without the advice of a physician, either directly or indirectly. The intent of the author is only to offer information of a general nature to help you in your quest for emotional and spiritual well-being. In the event you use any of the information in this book for yourself, which is your constitutional right, the author and the publisher assume no responsibility for your actions.

Any people depicted in stock imagery provided by Getty Images are models, and such images are being used for illustrative purposes only. Certain stock imagery © Getty Images.

Print information available on the last page.

ISBN (eBook):   978-1-956742-31-2
ISBN (Paperback):   978-1-662930-18-8

TO MY PARENTS, WHO CONTINUE TO SEND

ME WHISPERS OF INSPIRATION.

CONTENTS

Preface 1

Scatter seeds of kindness 2
The Weight of Memories 4
Stereotypes 7
The Bully 8
The Difference 15
My Bubble 18
Time - The Great Stealer 21
Mirror Image 23
Writer's Block 25
Reflections of the Day 27
Between Coffee and Wine 32
It's Winter Once Again 34
The Storm Inside 37
Cowboy Boots and Blue Jeans 39
My Therapist 42
Life Lessons outside the Classroom 44
Dreams 47
Ode to the Little Yellow Car 50
Life's Reward 52
Humble Pie 54
The Devil on my Shoulder 57
Time Spent with Friends 62
Every Day 65
Let Life Unfold 67
Pieces of Us 70
Scatter seeds of kindness 72

Acknowledgments 73
About the Author 75

PREFACE

Dear Reader,

First of all, thank you so much for picking up this book. I had such a great time putting together the poems and short stories for my first book, so I decided to do it again. I could not have done it without your kindness and support so it is fitting that this book has kindness in the title. It is a very scary undertaking to put your thoughts and words out into the world where people aren't always kind. But I have received so many positive comments and words of encouragement, so that took the fear and apprehension out of doing it all a second time!

My first book, *Walk Through a Field of Flowers*, was a compilation of poems collected over a lifetime, starting as a young girl with only a few new ones written in recent years. Most of the poems were deeply personal for many reasons, but mainly because I got to share them with my parents, and those are such great memories. I remember my dad's roaring laughter as I read an unexpected ending to a poem about a little mouse, or my mom sitting at the kitchen table, usually doing her nails and watching *Dynasty* on the little TV on the kitchen counter. She would always mute the TV (this was before the days of being able to pause live TV), and as I read my latest poem she would make a hand gesture with both hands, her fingers extended, palms down, signaling me to slow down. I still see that hand signal in my mind's eye every time I have to speak in front of a group of people.

This book is all new material, so even though I don't have the joy of sharing these poems with my parents, I treasure the opportunity to be able to share them with you. In here you will find some common themes such as memories and how they impact our life, the passage of time, stereotypes within society, as well as some heavier topics like bullying. However, there are some fun and lighthearted poems sprinkled in that will hopefully bring a smile to your face. I also share my own struggles with practicing kindness, and not always succeeding.

I hope you enjoy this new collection of poems and stories as I explain the inspiration, motivation, or sometimes just my random thoughts on each poem. I appreciate you taking the time to walk with me again through this new book.

SCATTER SEEDS OF KINDNESS

Wherever you may go.
Reach deep inside your heart
And scatter them to and fro.
Scatter seeds of kindness
And bring a few to share.
You never know when you'll find the chance
To show someone you care.
Scatter seeds of kindness
And watch them as they bloom.
A little good can go a long way
To chase away the gloom.
Someone may be hurting
And you can plant the seed;
A kind word or a smile
May be exactly what they need.
Scatter seeds of kindness
And hope others do the same.
A candle loses nothing
When it shares its glowing flame.

This poem has to do with memories and how they can shape us throughout our lives. How often have you heard a song on the radio or smelled a familiar smell and it brings you right back to a certain time and place, and suddenly you are lost, reminiscing? Memories are precious; they are the storybooks of our lives, and oftentimes they bring us together as we share stories that begin with "remember when …?"

How horrible it is when someone develops Alzheimer's, and their memory is gone—and how sad for their loved ones. Then one day, they pull something out of the memory bank and everyone is astonished and hopeful. But it doesn't last long, unfortunately, and before long the glassy stare into the distance is back and they are looking at you as if you were a stranger.

Memories work hand in hand with our conscience. If we are about to repeat a past mistake or something that did not work out so well, this tag team steps in, placing a little voice in our ear to remind us—and to hopefully get us to think twice about what we are about to do.

I have a drawer that I call my memory drawer. It is stuffed full with photo albums, loose pictures, birthday and other cards collected from friends and family throughout the years, memorial cards picked up at funerals for those who passed away, and various other trinkets and mementos. Many people hold onto these reminders of childhood, Christmases and holidays, birthday parties, prom, and so on. There are times I open the drawer intending to quickly look for something and I immediately get caught up in reading the cards or looking at some of the photo albums. It is bittersweet when this happens, as I look back on my life and the moments that were important enough that I held onto them in some form or another. Then there are other times when I am just struggling to get through today without dredging up the past, and I know that opening up that drawer is going to have to wait for another day.

I have found that memories can change over time. They can soften or become less emotional, or in some cases they can stir up old feelings of anger or betrayal. Suddenly an emotion you thought you had moved on from is back in your life again.

Sometimes we keep things running through our heads on a continuous loop over and over again on replay. What value is there in hanging onto these memories? What is the purpose of doing that, other than impacting the quality of your life in the present? If there is a lesson to be learned, learn it, apply it, and move on. If the nagging memory is due to a wrong that was done to someone, can an apology be made to rectify the situation and release the bad memory? If so, make it. But if there is nothing that can be done and all the memory does is bring you down, try to let it go. You cannot change the past, so why carry it around? Do not let it impact the present or carry it in the future. They all mesh together eventually, so don't let one impact the other in a negative way.

THE WEIGHT OF MEMORIES

There's a box of old memories
That sits up on a shelf.
I know exactly where it is,
I put it there myself.

There are times I go to reach for it
Then suddenly refrain.
Some days I'm just not strong enough
To walk down memory lane.

I don't know what I'll find there;
But then again I do.
Memories of days gone by;
The times I spent with you.

And many family photos
That reflect the happy years.
A good and carefree childhood,
Yet still there were some tears.

Who wants to open up old wounds?
Life is hard enough
Without reverting back in time
To all that gone-by stuff.

It is hard enough most days
To put a smile upon my face
Without dredging up old memories
Of a former time and place.

Memories are heavy,
They can weigh me down inside.
How long I choose to carry them,
Only I decide.

But memories are fluid,
They change as life goes by.
What once made me laugh with joy
Can now cause me to cry.

And quite the opposite, I find
Something that once caused tears
Can bring a smile to my face
As the pain, it disappears.

These memories, they are like clay;
They shape us as we grow.
They mold us as we take on life
With each experience that we sow.

These memories, they're building blocks
Stacking on each other.
Piece by piece, as life goes on
They build on one another.

They strengthen us so we stand tall
Against life's endless tide.
Each struggle that life brings forth
We can handle it in stride.

These memories, they are like trees
Standing tall and strong;
Allowing us to bend, not break
When hard times come along.

So whatever's in the box, don't fear,
It helped me shape and grow.
I can handle any memory …
And some I might let go.

So I'll go and open up that box
And honor what I find,
Because the present, past, and future
They all are intertwined.

This next poem has to do with the stereotypes put on us by society, and questions who are the ones who make these rules? Who gets to say that having a couple of cats makes you a crazy cat lady, but having a few dogs is perfectly acceptable? Where do these "rules" come from and how do they get ingrained in our culture? Society always has her claws out, scratching at our life. I talk more about society and its influence in our lives in upcoming poems.

This poem is meant to be lighthearted and a tribute to my love for all furry friends, no matter how many you have. But even I realize there is a limit, and when you take on too much of anything, something or someone will always suffer. So we always have to do what is in the best interest of the animal. In that, I am sure society would agree.

STEREOTYPES
(a.k.a. Crazy Cat Lady)

I have a friend who has three dogs
They live within her heart.
She cuddles them, she kisses them,
They rarely are apart.

When people see them walking by
They smile or stop to pet.
No one calls her crazy,
Or at least they haven't yet!

I have four cats that live with me,
Whom I love with all my heart.
I cuddle and I kiss them
And we rarely are apart.

But when people hear of my large brood
They shyly look away.
They don't want me to see their face
That says that I'm cray-cray!

So why is there the difference
Between our furry friends?
Who decides what's acceptable?
I guess that all depends.

Who decides these rules in life
And in society?
Why is someone smiled upon,
But others called crazy?

I don't need someone's judgment,
Nor in their eyes to see the pity.
There is nothing I'm ashamed of
Because I love a kitty (or four!).

Isn't it a better cause
To bring into a home
An animal that's safe and sound,
Instead of left to roam?

But one thing we have in common,
No matter what you love,
Be it dog or cat or hedgehog
Or even tiny turtle dove;

This one thing I am certain
And I boldly will proclaim,
When it's time for them to leave us
Our hearts break just the same.

THE BULLY

Throughout my youth and teenage years
I lived in the same town.
I had my small core group of friends;
I'd see other kids around.

Everyone seemed to get along
As well as most kids do.
If there were bullies lurking around the school,
I guess I never knew.

Then one day in my junior year
A new kid came to school.
He took up with the popular kids
And thought he was so cool.

One day in the classroom
He turned around to see
Me sitting in the back of class;
"The Beast" he nicknamed me.

From that day on, when we would pass
In the hallway or the yard,
"There goes the Beast," he'd loudly say.
It started to hit hard.

I'd hang my head when he approached
So he wouldn't notice me.
I prayed each night that when tomorrow came
He would just let me be.

I started to avoid the hall.
I'd rather be late for class
And go the long way around the school
Just to avoid this ass.

He'd poke his friends when I'd walk by;
"There goes the Beast," he'd say.
I'd pretend I had not heard him
As his friends all looked my way.

Then one night toward the end of May
A tragedy hit our town.
Two girls were killed in a deadly crash;
Our school turned upside down.

In the hallway students clung
In disbelief as they cried.
I'm sorry to say, the sister of the bully
Was one who died.

When the bully finally returned to school
He was a different guy.
Gone was the smirk across his face;
He shrunk when he walked by.

As he approached he no longer had
That confident, cocky swagger.
Instead he looked so very lost,
His footsteps would stumble and stagger.

Then one day in the hallway
Our gazes met at last.
"I'm sorry for your loss," I whispered
Quietly as I passed.

He nodded to me, a silent thanks,
No further words were spoken.
The pain he felt was palpable;
He really seemed quite broken.

From that day on, no longer did
He set his sights on me.
"The Beast" nickname he penned me
Was no longer meant to be.

Now looking back years later,
I wonder what I did
To have been given such a hateful name
From this troubled, insecure kid.

I know I did not deserve his scorn
But then, to be fair
He didn't deserve the loss he got,
And I know I can't compare.

But one hurt doesn't erase the other.
You can't undo the pain.
Although obtained in different ways,
The scars, they still remain.

Normally, I put the explanation of the poem first, as an introduction and to share my thoughts or inspiration. For this poem, I did not want the reader to see the tragedy coming or how the bully was impacted by this turn of events. I wanted the reader to feel the shock and surprise as the story unfolded, similar to the surprise someone might feel when a bully first makes them his or her target and the victim does not see it coming. The victim is just going about his or her day, and suddenly someone decides to strike at them and it throws them off course. I wanted to take the reader through the emotions of that, and then through the emotions of the bully as his life changed forever. This is a true story. Those that I grew up with might recognize the bully, but I will never admit who it was as to protect his "innocence."

Was this a story about karma? When I first started writing it that was my intention. I even had the line picked out for the ending: "Karma is a bitch and she knows where you live." But then as I relived the story and felt the emotions, I knew this was not karma at work. This kid did not deserve what happened to his family. This was a tragedy; no other words to describe it. He probably wasn't even a bad person at the core. Like most bullies, his words and actions were most likely due to being troubled and insecure, as most bullies are, and maybe he felt as if he could raise himself up by lowering others down.

That being said, I did not deserve to be targeted. No one does. This hurt beyond measure when it was happening, and often left me confused and withdrawn. I was just going about my day when someone decided to label me. How do we respond to that label we are given by others, and how does that shape and shift our life? When I was reliving the story, of course the hurt was still there, but it had lessened, and was not nearly as raw. In my earlier poem "The Weight of Memories," I talk about how memories are fluid, and how they change over time. Things that once hurt to the core may have softened, and memories that were good at the time may bring heartbreak or anger years later. I guess this is called perspective. But the fact that I still carry this memory around thirty plus years later tells me that how people treat you, and how you treat people matters. It did then and it does today. You never know how your words or even how you look at someone will impact their life, and how long they will carry it around with them.

One thing that still puzzles me, in this day and age, is why there is still so much bullying. Kids these days are taught much more tolerance than my generation was. Kids are taught to be accepting of each other, including those who are overweight, or gay or transgender, or come from families with people who are. Yet, we hear stories all the time of bullying and it is still a big problem in schools. Why are kids still so mean to each other? Is it just human nature, or a rite of passage into adulthood? I have witnessed cyberbullying by adults and it is brutal. People online could be involved in a discussion or posting their opinion about something relatively benign, and some anonymous person will come along and rip them to shreds just for having a different opinion or viewpoint. These cyberbullies have courage because they are hiding behind a keyboard and a computer screen. But would they ever speak to the person that way face-to-face? People who have gone on reality dating shows have had their lives turned upside down by other people combing through their social media to find a "controversial" post that the person may have inadvertently liked; or maybe they really did like the post, and that should be their choice. But these cyberbullies have ruined the person's life, including sending death threats, and have also gone after their families and tried to ruin them too, but for what? What is there to gain by ruining someone else's life over a TV show or a difference of opinion on a social media post?

The last verse of the poem assumes that the bully still has some pain and scars from the loss of his sister. I am sure this is true, especially since I am also carrying scars from that year. I was in no way trying to imply that being called a horrible name compares to the loss of a loved one; just that pain comes to each of us in different ways, and years later it still impacts our lives. I am not sure where the bully is in his life. I have not attempted to find him on social media, nor will I, and he has never been to any high school reunions that I have attended. I hope if he was blessed with children, that he taught them to be good and kind people, and that they do not need to break others down to lift themselves up. And I sincerely hope that they were never the target of a bully.

Are you familiar with Robert Frost's classic poem "The Road Not Taken"? In this poem, a traveler comes to a fork in the road and must make a decision; to take the path that is showing more wear, or the path that appears to be less traveled. In the end he decides to take the road less traveled, proclaiming later that it has made all the difference. This poem resonates with me because I feel as if I have taken a "less traveled" road, at least in society's eyes. Most people aspire to go to college, find a suitable spouse, settle down and raise a family. This is all very admirable and I would never say there is anything wrong with that. It is just not anything I ever wished for. I am not opposed to getting married, I just never dreamed about it. I never called myself a princess or donned a fake wedding gown to play "Bride." I never envisioned what my husband would be like or felt the instinct to have a baby. The thought of planning a wedding sounded dreadful to me. I used to say, if I was to ever get married, I wanted to pick out the dress. That was it. Well, that and the groom too! Other than that, just tell me where to be and what time and I would show up. So marriage was not in the cards for me and I am OK with that. I have always been a bit of a loner, and when I was a kid I used to love it when my parents and siblings would go out for the evening, and I would have all of that precious time and space to myself! I would do my ninety-minute Jane Fonda aerobic workout without anyone watching or making fun, then pop some popcorn and watch a betamax movie; probably *St. Elmo's Fire* for the hundredth time, relishing all that silence with no one around to comment on the cheesy parts of the movie.

But this way of life does not mesh with society's expectations. In my opinion, our society has a better view of people who are divorced than of people who have never been married. I have heard people say that if a person is divorced, at least they tried. But if someone has never been married, the label put on a person is never positive. They are called a commitment-phobe, or people wonder what is wrong with them. Why has no one wanted them thus far? Women are labeled as the horrific "spinster," while men get to be known as a "bachelor", but even that comes with the same types of questions and raised eyebrows, so they too are not off the hook. But again, who decides? No one considers that maybe this was their own choice.

I am sure newly married couples who want to remain childless often feel the same way, with people always asking them when they are going to start a family. Or if they decide they only want one or two children, they are constantly asked when the next one is coming. Even more upsetting is when a couple is trying with everything they have to start a family and it is just not happening, yet the questions still keep coming. How awful for these hopeful parents to always have to explain that they are still trying. I discuss stereotypes again in my poems "Stereotypes—(a.k.a. Crazy Cat Lady") and "My Bubble," so it is a running theme throughout this book.

People are not always sure how to respond to someone like me. When they ask if I have ever been married and I say no, often they will shrug and say "Oh, well that's OK," because they really don't know how else to respond. I have learned to live with these off-the-cuff remarks, and I give some leeway because I know that I am somewhat of an enigma. I know it is okay, and I know I am okay and that there is nothing wrong with me because I chose the less worn path. The traveler and I have that in common.

THE DIFFERENCE

"The Road Not Taken" by Robert Frost
Is my favorite poem.
It speaks to me so much
I have it hanging in my home.

In the poem the wandering traveler
Has a choice to make.
Whichever path he chooses
He has something to forsake.

I've chosen to take a less traveled road
Than many would desire.
Marriage was not in my path,
Nor did I aspire

To live the more traditional life
Of home and family.
A loner to the core, I am;
This life works best for me.

I crave my solitude most days,
And yet there's still that fear
That fate will call my bluff someday,
And all will disappear.

And I will be left truly alone
Regretting choices that I made.
I'll die alone as I have lived;
The proverbial old maid.

Like the traveler in the poem
Who had to pick a lane,
He took the road less traveled.
As for me, I did the same.

I hope it worked out well for him,
As I hope it does for me.
Has it made all the difference?
I guess we'll wait and see.

When most people hear that someone is an introvert, they may picture someone alone, maybe curled up on the couch with a book while the extroverts are out partying. I read somewhere that being an introvert or an extrovert has to do with where a person gets their energy from, i.e., their ability to recharge. An introvert would tend to recharge or regroup by spending time alone, whereas an extrovert recharges by being social and around other people, and can actually have their energy sapped or drained if they spend too much time alone. This was particularly interesting to me as I sometimes feel as if I could be either depending on the situation. There are times when I can be very social and chatty with everyone, or other times where I can be quiet and a little withdrawn, sometimes in the same evening or event. Well, imagine my surprise to learn recently that there is a third personality trait; an ambivert. This is someone who exhibits qualities of both an introvert and extrovert at different times, and can switch from an introvert to an extrovert depending on their mood, situation, and people around them. This describes me to a "T". I used to just think I was moody if I was in a social setting and I felt my energy levels decrease and my desire to get home increase. Now I know I was just switching from being an extrovert back to being an introvert. I think ambivert is a much better description than moody!

This next poem carries on the theme of being a loner and secluding oneself away from society. In the previous poem "The Difference," I referred to myself as a loner to the core. That is not entirely true. I am probably more of a loner than most people and I do really need my "alone time" at least a few times a week. This is where I recharge my energy levels. But I also enjoy social time, and I often really yearn for time with friends to unwind and catch up, and that also allows me to reenergize. However, too much of either one and I start to feel the anxiety kick in as I crave the opposite, and I feel a little unsettled until I get either the social activity or the solitude that my soul is asking for. As I mentioned in "The Difference," I don't want fate to call my bluff and take everyone away from me because it thinks I want to be alone in the world. That is not the case at all. I love my friends and family very much but still do need that time away from everyone to indulge in some solitude and let my soul renew.

Recent events have caused many of us to want to hide inside and not come out. During the COVID-19 pandemic, when the majority of states issued a stay-at-home order in March 2020, most everyone that could comply did (the exception being health care and essential workers). However, the longer it went on, the more people got restless from being locked inside and kept away from social events, family parties, weddings, and even funerals, unfortunately. Not that anyone could blame them. The lockdown was extending into summertime, and if you know Chicago weather, that season is very short. However, I rather enjoyed being home, inside my bubble as I started to call it. Then, toward the end of May the civil unrest in the country began, and provided even more reasons to not want to step outside into the craziness of the world. These days, with online shopping and food deliveries both from grocery stores and restaurants with the assistance of companies like Amazon, Peapod, DoorDash, and Grubhub, a person could essentially live inside for a very long time without any reason to come outside into the world. This way of living might keep us safe, but is it keeping us healthy? Many people experienced elevated anxiety, depression, and loneliness during the lockdown, not to mention missing opportunities to indulge in some fresh air and sunshine. In some cases this led to increases in alcohol and drug use, as well as suicides and divorces. It is not only the pandemic that caused people to want to stay inside and hide. As I have mentioned a few times, our culture does embrace certain stereotypes, and many people do not feel as if they belong within these confines that have been set. If someone feels that they are "different" or do not belong, that may cause them to hide inside their bubble and isolate themselves from a society that does not quite understand them.

As inviting as it might sound to live inside a bubble, the truth is that we cannot hide away from the world if we want to live a healthy and satisfying life. Even the person in this poem realizes that they miss the companionship of others, and eventually they invite someone inside with them. Hopefully, in time, they will find the courage to step out of their bubble and back into the real world.

MY BUBBLE

I live inside my bubble
And it's where I want to be.
It's cozy and it's comfy
And no harm can come to me.

The virus cannot find me
And the flu won't buzz my door.
The cold bug doesn't bother
To try to find me anymore.

I live inside my bubble
And it's where I choose to hide.
The shootings and the chaos
Can all carry on outside.

> The road rage and the anger
> Won't get the best of me
> As I live inside my bubble
> Just as happy as can be.
>
> Inside my little bubble
> I am who I choose to be
> Without worries of the judgments
> That come from society.
>
> But one thing about my bubble,
> And I'm sure you will agree
> The only company I keep
> Is just myself and me.
>
> So sometimes I get lonely
> And I start missing you,
> But good news is that my bubble
> Has room enough for two!

As I get older I am so much more aware of how quickly time is passing by. My mother used to warn me about that, when I used to pester her every day in December asking if it was Christmas yet, because it seemed like it would *never* arrive! Or think of those car trips … "Are we there yet? Are we there yet?" Now it is crazy how fast the years go by. I really see the passage of time when I look at my nieces and nephew, or other people's children. How is it that this little child, who was just in diapers, is graduating college or having children of their own? I sometimes wish life had a pause button and we could just stop the scene and take it all in before hitting PLAY and watching the chaos unfold again.

Time is often referred to as a healer or as some type of deity, as if it will provide all the answers eventually. People are told that time heals all wounds, or when someone is pondering something, they are told to "give it time." There is value in both thoughts. I have had situations where I was undecided about what to do so I "gave it time" and sure enough, I received some clarity which helped me make a decision. I tend to be a bit of a compulsive person, so giving things time does help to reel in those impulses to act immediately. The theory of waiting can work in reverse too. Sometimes if we take too long to make a decision the opportunity might be gone and we have lost out. Time is finicky. It is like an avocado; you have to gauge when it is at its finest in order to reap the benefits. Act too soon and you might have had a better result if you'd waited a day or two. But wait too long and the chance you have been waiting for may have turned to mush.

Does time heal all wounds? I am not sure if heal is the right word. I believe time softens things, and makes them more bearable. If you lose someone you loved I don't think you ever get over them. You just learn to live with it and go on. Time helps with that but it doesn't cure the ache, it just makes it a little duller each year.

But more often than not, time just seems to take away from us. For most of us, it takes our looks, it takes our strength and health, and in some unfortunate cases it takes our memories. I wrote about this in my earlier poem "The Weight of Memories." I suppose if it wasn't for time we would not have those memories to reflect back on and see how wonderful our life has been. People who are battling a terminal illness would give anything for more time, and their loved ones would give anything for more time with them. As much as we try to not be so obsessed with time, how can we not be? It impacts every aspect of our life. As the saying goes, "The days are long, but the years are short."

TIME - THE GREAT STEALER

When my father passed away one night
My mother cried and cried
About all the things they never did or saw
before he died.

"There wasn't time to do it all"
I'd often hear her fret;
"He's gone too soon, I need more time
It can't be over yet."

Tick Tock Tick Tock, we are obsessed
With those numbers on the dial.
The calendar we flip from month to month
in some denial.

We deny how fast it's slipping by
As snow melts into rain.
We cut the grass, kids trick or treat,
It's snowing once again.

Fast forward thirty years or so,
The kids are grown and gone.
My mother's life is near its end
It doesn't seem that long …

Since she cooked for us, and cared for us
And sent us off to school.
Damn time, it rears its head again;
It really is quite cruel.

Fast forward just a few more months,
A rainy, dreary day;
I laid in bed and held her hand
As she slowly slipped away.

I saw the nurse checking her watch
To call the time of death.
"Damn time, you stole from me again"
I said under my breath.

Perhaps I need a change of heart,
For time can be a healer.
But as I watch the years slip right on by
It just seems like a stealer.

I know I should be grateful
for all the time we get.
But still I think, it's gone too fast,
It can't be over yet.

The previous poem talked about my mom and how distraught she was at my dad's sudden passing in 1989. We were all shocked and devastated, but I will never forget her strength as she gathered us kids around the kitchen table that morning and said, "we will get through this." I often heard her tell people that she got through it because she had us kids, but I believe that we kids got through it because we had her. One image I don't think I will ever get out of my head is that of my mom leaving the funeral home the day that the family was allowed some time to say our "final" goodbyes. My mom left that room on my brother's arm, standing tall, shoulders back, only the tears streaming down her face giving any clue to her pain. I remember thinking, "That is grace under pressure." I don't show that kind of strength and grace on my best day, and yet she was able to show it on her worst.

This next poem is a shout-out to all of the amazing women I know who have displayed such strength over the years. Whether it was raising amazing children, dealing with aging parents (sometimes both at the same time), having a career, dealing with illness (your own or someone close to you), this goes out to you. You know who you are.

MIRROR IMAGE

Who is that woman
standing tall and strong;
The one who can face anything
When hard times come along?

Who is that woman
Who can take on any task,
And will always lend a helping hand
If only you just ask?

Who is that woman
Who wipes her child's tears
And makes scrapbooks of their memories
To capture all the years?

Who is that woman
With eyes that shed a tear
But whose stance won't give her pain away,
Or any hint of fear?

Who is that woman
Who never needs direction?
Guess what? It's you ... You're in the mirror.
That is your own reflection.

I almost called this next poem "The struggle is real," because it is! Writer's block has been discussed and dissected for several years and it is a true phenomenon. What causes writer's block and how do writers get over it? I don't have all of those answers, but I can share my experience. When I was younger I used to write poems and short stories all the time. My childhood BFF Tina and I would constantly pass our notebooks back and forth, reading what the other had written, and we lived for Creative Writing class. Many of these poems were shared in my first book, *Walk Through a Field of Flowers*. Apart from one or two poems, most of these were written in the 1990s. After that, all of the writing stopped. It was as if the well ran dry. To be honest, I really hadn't noticed much that I had stopped writing. From time to time someone would ask me if I had written anything new and the answer was always the same; nothing recently. In my first book, I wrote about how the COVID-19 shutdown had led me to rediscover my forgotten binder with all my poems inside, and from there I was able to put them together into a compilation, which became my first book. I did write a few new poems last year, including one called "The Middle," about how the COVID-19 shutdown was impacting those people (mainly women, but men were impacted too) who suddenly had to deal with kids being home from school, and online learning, while also trying to hold down a job in the new "Work from Home" world. I also wrote about the civil unrest that took place in 2020. So, these couple of things, inspired by recent events, told me I still had something left inside to write. I wasn't finished yet.

Lately, to deal with all the stress and anxiety due to everything going on in the world, I have been focusing on some stress relief techniques, including meditation and EFT (Emotional Freedom Techniques) tapping. I won't get into the techniques. There are plenty of meditation and tapping apps out there to check into. These are things that I used to think were just hooey, but I have been doing a tapping meditation every night and suddenly the words are flowing again. So, is there something to this, or just coincidence? I am not sure. Stress can wreak havoc on us in so many ways, so if these meditation techniques are helping to relieve some of the stress and unblock whatever it was that had brought my writing to a halt, I am all for it. A big fear for any writer is that the words will stop again and they will be staring at a blank page for hours on end, so I am going to keep doing what I am doing and hopefully the words will keep on flowing.

Incidentally, this poem talks about how sometimes the words are everywhere. I love it when that happens but it can become distracting. Last weekend I was doing some chores and had to keep stopping to jot down this thought or that. I have had to exit a shower early just to get that verse down that I have been toying with all morning, and then suddenly there it is, just when I put the conditioner in my hair! I have to get these thoughts onto paper right away or unfortunately they're gone. I do keep a pen and paper next to my bed just in case something wakes me up in the middle of the night. In my first book, there is a poem called "Inspiration" where I talk about standing in line in grocery stores and texting myself words or lines that pop into my head. I always use paper, as an upcoming poem mentions, but I will take advantage of modern technology when I have the chance. The writing process can be so rewarding when I get it just right, but there is a lot of time spent just searching and searching, and that is the frustrating side. Sometimes I just need to leave it alone and let the thought marinate in my brain for a few days and then suddenly there it is, what I have been searching for! But like I mentioned above, I have to get it down quickly or it is gone. So, I will take the words following me all around over the struggle to find them at all, as long as they don't start to become voices in my head!

WRITER'S BLOCK

I hope that I can write today.
I hope the words do flow.
Some days they're like a river,
Other days they refuse to show.

It is frustrating to look down and see
A page empty and white,
When words are jumbled in my head
But I just can't get them right.

I know the words I want to write;
What I'm trying to convey.
But for some reason they don't come out right,
Maybe save for another day?

Then other times my mind is blank,
The words are stuck, not flowing.
No matter where I look for sparks
I just can't get them going.

That is the most frustrating of all.
It is like I'm stuck in time,
And then a word pops in my head
And I search for a suitable rhyme.

Once I get it going
A story unfolds from there.
Suddenly all around me,
Words are everywhere!

They follow me to the shower
They join me in my bed.
I keep a pad and pen around
Just to remove them from my head.

They nag me when I'm driving
And they follow me back home.
The words are bouncing in my head;
They won't leave me alone!

It sounds like that's a problem
But it's really not at all.
I'm thankful when this happens
For it's much better than the stall.

On those such days when I am stuck
I must admit defeat.
But today I'm grateful that I wrote,
And allowed pen and pad to meet!

REFLECTIONS OF THE DAY

From dawn to dusk, the words they flow
Inside my tired head;
The things I did, the things I thought,
Those things I left unsaid.

Or words I spoke with tongue too harsh
That struck out of the blue;
The look you gave, the hurtful eyes,
What made me strike at you?

The road rage on the way to work,
The hurdles in my way,
Pedestrians stuck in my path,
The train that caused delay,

The frustration as it builds and grows
Stuck in an intersection;
A glance into the rearview mirror
I see my own reflection.

It's tense and angry—where's the joy
to live another day?
Too many thoughts roam through my head
To chase that joy away.

Then suddenly I see it hit,
The car that ran the light!
The crash, the BOOM, the breaking glass;
I tense in "fight or flight."

Then sigh and breathe, it was not me.
I'm safe, out of the path.
I take a moment, say a prayer,
I'm spared this awful wrath.

Someone's life just changed forever
before my very eyes.
The chaos as the scene unfolds,
The desperate, anguished cries;

The sirens blaring through the air
Take me back to reality.
Three seconds sooner had I approached,
I knew this could be me.

My fingers grip the steering wheel;
My heart pounds through my chest.
I slowly exit from the scene
As my brain tries to digest.

I reflect upon the day thus far,
My thoughts so negative;
When others suffer greater strife
Yet have such will to live.

I am annoyed by such small things
That I let impact my day.
I take to heart, to my own harm,
Things that get in my way.

They slow me down, distract my mind
And throw my day off course.
But perhaps there is a lesson there
From some greater, unseen force.

I say a silent "thank you."
For some reason I was spared.
My heart goes out to those today
Whose lives were so impaired.

I vow to turn my thoughts around,
Embrace the positive
And wave away bad energy,
Life has too much to give.

But as I learn to walk down this new path
I know I'll trip and fall.
Bad thoughts will creep into my head;
I am human, after all.

So reflecting on this, at the end of the day
I promise to do my best.
But for now, it has been quite a day
So I'll allow myself to rest.

This is another poem where I chose to put my thoughts after the poem, so that the reader would not see the crash coming. Ironically, I did not see that crash coming either. This poem started off with someone at the end of the day just recalling all the frustrating and mundane events that happened. The poem was going to be about how the person was feeling bad about the way she treated loved ones, and how she let little things throughout the day eat away at her and steal her joy and goodwill. Then suddenly, before I even knew what was happening, I was writing the car crash verse. So this poem went in an entirely different direction than I had planned, which is fitting I suppose, because how many times does our day end up going in an entirely different direction than we had planned when we woke up?

Some people believe that there are no coincidences and that everything happens for a reason. I imagine one of those bird's-eye view scenes in a movie of a large city and everyone going about their day, in and out of coffee shops, bumping into each other, darting in and out of traffic, etc. It all seems so random, yet we are supposed to believe that there is a reason that everyone is at that same time and place? The concept of "no coincidences" seems far-fetched to me. But if there are no coincidences, what does that say when or if something bad happens to you? What is the universe trying to tell you? If it wasn't a coincidence, did you do something to deserve this bad luck? Is there a lesson that you are supposed to learn from this incident happening in your life? In this poem, the woman was thankfully spared the bad luck, but she did learn something just by witnessing it. This person was able to take an introspective look and realize how she was letting events that happen throughout the day chip away at her, and ultimately her happiness and good nature. It was impacting her relationship with others, as she replayed in her mind the way she spoke to her loved ones. She realized that there are people in the world who are suffering in much greater ways than being stopped by a train or running late for an appointment, and yet they have such strength and perseverance to continue fighting each day. In the end she vows to try to do better but realizes that she is human and will probably have some failings. Perhaps that is the reason she was placed at the scene rather than being directly involved. Just being an observer to an event is sometimes enough to get a point across and therefore, as in this case, it was not a coincidence that she was there at that exact time. Sometimes we don't need a large jolt when just a small nudge will prove the point.

How many times do we witness something or hear about someone else's misfortune and we hold our breath and say a few prayers; one to pray for the person or family impacted, and a second to say thanks that it didn't happen to us? In that moment we vow to do better, be kinder, and give more; whether it is love, or money, or time. But then the next day rolls around and we start our day and something happens to throw us off and the cycle continues again, the reflection from the previous night forgotten as we go about our day, already haggard. As the person in this poem eventually realizes, she is just human and trying her best. Perhaps at the end of the day, realizing and understanding that we are all works in progress and just aspiring to do better is the most important reflection of all.

A friend had posted a meme on social media with coffee brewing, and it said *"Perkatory (noun): The prolonged and anguishing period of time spent waiting for a fresh pot of coffee."* Isn't that the truth?! I live for my coffee in the morning and my wine in the evening. But what do we do with all that time in between? I am not someone who wants to see time rush past, as I feel it goes by fast enough already, as I mentioned in my earlier poem about how time is a stealer. However, there are days (OK, most days) when I just cannot wait for the day to end so I can pour myself that delicious glass of wine. It is such a treat at the end of the day. It is not every day, but I do enjoy a glass when I am making dinner or when I go out to lunch or socially on the weekends. Then, the next morning, I rely on my beloved coffee to once again get me through the day and do it all again.

I remember when I was in my early 20s and my coworkers and I would drag ourselves through the workday envisioning quitting time when we could rush home and take a nap. But for some reason, when that time came, we suddenly found ourselves reenergized and would head to the local bar and grill for Happy Hour. This "hour" frequently extended into 1:00 or 2:00 a.m., and we would catch a few hours sleep and then pull ourselves through yet another workday with (thankfully) our much-appreciated coffee to carry us through. We usually had to hold each other up as the afternoon sleepiness would set in. But guess what? Five p.m. would roll in and suddenly there we were, ready to do it all again.

Nowadays, I cannot fathom staying out that late even one night a week and then heading to work the next day on only a few hours sleep. As Mark Twain once said, "Too bad that youth is wasted on the young." Well, my youth might be gone, but fortunately I still have my coffee!

BETWEEN COFFEE AND WINE

I stumble to the kitchen
Where it's waiting every day.
Just one push of a button
And liquid Heaven comes my way.

Drip-Drip-Drip it takes too long,
I'm in Perkatory;
The time until the coffee's done,
Then I'll be in my glory.

Neither cream nor sugar do I need;
All that just takes time.
As long as steam is flowing out
I'll drink it black just fine!

The warmth as it floats past my lips
And warms me to my core,
The brain fog lifting with each sip
I just need one cup more!

Then onto my day with head now clear,
The hours tick on past.
I log off work and grab my coat,
It's five o'clock at last!

Choices! Choices! What to have …
A dry red or crisp white?
I settle on a sweet rosé
It's chilled and tastes just right.

I'll have one more or maybe two …
Then I switch to a dry red.
Big mistake—I should have stopped
As I stumble to my bed.

A restless night, an early dawn
I cringe at my behavior;
But stumble to the kitchen
To greet coffee—my great savior!

As an avid reader, I've always loved when I read books from the same author and they bring back a character from a previous book. It is like seeing an old friend and catching up. In my previous book, there is a poem called "It's Springtime Once Again." In that poem, Mother Earth is just waking up from her winter's nap and kicking away all the winter dreariness. The babbling brook is talking away to the breeze, the chipmunks are running up and down the trees, and the kids are out flying a kite. They are all out enjoying the rebirth of the spring season.

This next poem is a prequel to that poem. All of those characters are here, except they are all hunkered down for winter. I hope you enjoy visiting with them again!

IT'S WINTER ONCE AGAIN

An icicle hangs outside my window,
The world is bathed in white.
The howling wind sings a mournful tune,
No bird would dare take flight.

I feel the chill deep in my bones.
Old Man Winter has arrived.
He's frigid and he's angry,
And he leaves me warmth deprived.

I feel it right down to my core
That winter's in the air.
My breath comes out in blasts of white,
There are snowflakes in my hair.

Mother Earth's gone back to sleep.
She's snuggled warm and tight.
Even she can't bear the chill
on this cold December night.

She pulls the blanket past her eyes
And covers up her head.
She'll see us in a few long months
When she steps out of her bed.

The chipmunks are all hunkered down
With their precious haul
Of all the nuts and acorns
That they gathered in the fall.

The babbling brook is frozen still.
She has no words to say.
I'm sure she will make up for it
when thawing comes our way.

The trees enjoy the quiet
As they stand so proud and bare.
The silence of the little brook
Is something that's quite rare.

I see the children bundled up
Sledding down the hill.
Faster, faster, there they go!
Their laughter is so shrill.

It won't be long 'til they go inside
To warm themselves back up
Where Mama will be waiting
With heated chocolate in a cup.

Despite the frigid cold,
There is magic in the air.
The snowflakes look like crystals,
And there's beauty everywhere!

Once again it strikes my soul
How much I love this place
As I wrap my arms around the world
Into a warm embrace.

I know that I'll be warm again
But I can't imagine when.
So I'll just count the days
Until it's springtime once again!

This next poem was one I found unfinished in my binder of poems that I had been reunited with last year. I am pretty sure that all those years ago I intended it to be a story of a young romance that had ended, and now the person was reflecting back, remembering the sweet joy of young love. As I started to play around with it, once again the words took me in a different direction, and this turned into a story about two young people who were separated in a terrible way. We never know what life is going to throw at us, and these two young lovers clearly had no idea of the real storm that was headed their way.

This is another reminder to cherish every day with our loved ones, because we never know what storm is brewing inside of us to sweep it all away. I also think it is important to note that almost everyone is fighting some kind of internal battle. It might not be a terminal illness, but most people do have some inner conflict or struggle that they are dealing with, or regrets about past mistakes or decisions. In my earlier poem, "The Weight of Memories," I discuss how memories are heavy and can weigh us down, but that we each need to decide just how long to carry them around before we release them into the world and remove the burden from ourselves.

So many people are struggling, and sometimes it is obvious; whether physical or emotional you can see it all over their faces. Then there are others who are so good at hiding their pain. Cats are like this. They don't let you know they are sick until it is almost too late to help them, because to show their illness makes them weaker to a predator. Is that what some people think; that revealing pain is a sign of weakness? I definitely don't think it is. Then there are the people who complain about *everything*! You know who I am talking about; the people whom you have stopped asking how they are doing because they will tell you every little detail and all about every ache and pain. As they say in the south, "Bless their heart."

My friend's dad used to talk about the "Pile of Problems." He would say that if everyone threw their problems into a pile, each person would grab back their own problem after seeing what the others are dealing with, because once you see what someone else is struggling with, sometimes your problem doesn't seem that bad.

Pain comes in many shapes and forms; sometimes physical, sometimes emotional, and sometimes it is past pain carried into the present, perhaps triggered by a memory that the person suddenly cannot shake. So it is good to give people some leeway and bring out the kindness whenever we can. I write this as a reminder to myself also, as I am not always kind when I should be. I lose my patience in traffic and honk and swear at people more than I should. I turn away from people holding signs at intersections asking for assistance. I get irritated if someone cuts in line at the grocery store, or if I am waiting in a long line and a new register opens and someone new walks right on up. Sometimes I say something, but more often than not I let it fester inside of me and then I carry it into my day by being irritated and unkind to others. I know my thoughts and actions don't always exemplify what I am encouraging here. But sometimes just being aware, and realizing that we are human and trying to do the best we can, is a step forward in the right direction.

THE STORM INSIDE

I remember the night we watched the storm
Your arms around me, safe and warm
My head against your sturdy arm
I thought nothing could do us harm.
I remember listening to the rain
That drip-drop-drip-drop sweet refrain
The lightening as it lit the skies
Left us silent, mesmerized.
What kind of thoughts went through your head
As we watched the storm with words unsaid?
Storms that test the strength of spirit
Wondering if I could bear it

A life without you by my side
As you fought the battle that raged inside.
One small cell that had created
An enemy that quickly invaded
Your body; fighting an unknown force
Throwing both our lives off course.
Month by month you grew too thin
As you fought the enemy within.
I remember my tears as I cried and cried
While you stood strong against the tide.
Eight months later you lost the fight
Slipping away into the night.

Now many years later I hear the rain
That drip-drop-drip-drop sweet refrain
My thoughts return to those days carefree
Before we learned of this enemy.
The rain, it always takes me back
To the days before this deadly attack
That time, so innocent and pure;
I pray some day they find a cure.

This is a fun little poem that was inspired by today's new country music. I really do like the new sounds coming out of Nashville these days. They're much lighter than the country music of the past, where the singer lost his job, and his wife, and his dog. Many people enjoy the music, but I really love the lyrics, which are really just poetry set to song. Johnny Cash's "Ragged Old Flag" is really just spoken word, but the words and they way he speaks them in the song are so powerful.

Unlike the person in this poem, I would never advise anyone else on how to dress, what kind of car to drive, etc. I have had men that I dated in the past do that to me. They would say "You know, you would look better if …," or "Have you ever thought about doing …," fill in the blank. It could be growing my hair longer or cutting it shorter, wearing different clothes, and so on. I've even had men comment on my perfume. I used to love wearing White Shoulders back in the '90s. Evidently the men I dated loved it too, telling me that I smelled so good, I reminded them of their grandmother. After the third man told me that, I finally got the hint and in the trash it went.

Truth be told, I really am a T-shirt and jeans kind of gal, so it is no surprise that I would be drawn to the same kind of man. And those cowboy boots do drive me a little crazy!

COWBOY BOOTS AND BLUE JEANS

I love a man dressed in a suit,
He always looks so fine.
I won't say no to surf and turf,
That surely sounds divine!

But you can keep your fancy suit
And your fancy wheels.
I sure don't need Armani
To give me all the feels.

You can show up in a Porsche
But I prefer a Jeep,
Or a rugged, muddy pickup truck
If you want my heart to keep.

You can don your skinny jeans;
I guess that is a start.
But cowboy boots and blue jeans
Are the ways to win my heart.

If you show up on a Harley
You'll really make me swoon.
Throw on a faded flannel shirt
And I just might hit the moon.

Put on some Metallica
And my heart belongs to you,
Especially in those cowboy boots
And those jeans of blue.

The fancy things, they don't impress
So don't even waste my time.
I'm happy with an ice cold beer,
But I do enjoy my wine!

I'm really just a simple girl
I don't require much.
For me, I find more value
In your words and in your touch.

So treat me right and with respect
And I'll be good to you.
But it wouldn't hurt to throw on those boots
And those jeans of blue.

When I was in about fifth grade my parents bought me my very own diary! It had a lock and everything and I couldn't wait to start writing in it. At first, I wrote every night, detailed information about the day's activities. Then slowly the diary and the chore of writing in it started to lose its novelty. I stopped writing anything about my feelings or my thoughts. It was all very objective: Went to school, ate a ham sandwich, talked to Keith on the bus. That was about the extent of it. It went downhill from there, as in every day that followed, I would literally write "same as yesterday." Oh, what a dull life! It was only when I sat down to write a poem, and to string words together that rhymed and created a story, that writing held any interest for me.

As I got older and started reading some self-help books (OK, a lot of them), journaling was mentioned in so many of them as a form of therapy. As I mentioned in the earlier poem "Writer's Block," I have recently taken up some relaxation techniques such as meditation and EFT tapping, but still to this day journaling just does not hold any interest for me. I am still not interested in writing down my feelings and thoughts on paper (and I'm even less interested in talking about them!). But I still do love recreational writing, and all these years later stringing words together still gives me a thrill. I still use paper to write, in lieu of modern technology, although I will revert to technology if I am in a situation where pulling out pen and paper is not practical. I really enjoy putting pen to paper, and I have even gone back to an old school planner, after my fancy calendar on my phone failed to notify me more than once of an upcoming appointment. That being said, there is a certain satisfaction that comes from writing a to-do list, or putting a task in your calendar. It is like making a commitment to yourself that you will get something done. Even greater satisfaction is crossing that task off your list when it is complete. Remember how in grade school we used to get marks for penmanship? Even though my handwriting was atrocious, and seemed to get worse as I got older, writing in cursive taught lessons on how to be detailed and organized with our thoughts, because we couldn't just backspace or hit the Edit>Undo button. I find it a shame that kids are no longer taught cursive in most schools. It is such a beautiful method to communicate.

A friend asked me awhile back if writing poetry for me is a way to embrace reality, or a distraction from it. In many ways it is both. I use current events as inspiration, as in the poems in my first book that discussed COVID-19 or the civil unrest of 2020, or my poem about 9/11. But it is not just current news events that can inspire. Inspiration is everywhere if you just look around. My friend's wedding, my father's death, listening to country music, even the change of seasons are all very real situations that can inspire words to flow. But I also do use writing as a way to escape. Just recently, while writing these new poems for this book, I turned off the news and listened to more music for motivation. So that took me away from the real world for awhile, and honestly, I am OK with that, because by now we could probably all use a break!

This poem is for all of those people who have embraced journaling as a form of therapy and recreation. And the best part? Your paper won't tell your secrets to anyone!

MY THERAPIST

My paper is my healer,
I write all my feelings down.
It helps to get them off my mind
Where they just bounce around.

My paper is my therapist;
There's no fear that it will judge.
And if I write something offensive
It doesn't hold a grudge.

My paper, it holds all my thoughts
Some are simple, some are deep,
But I always know my paper
Will all my secrets keep.

My paper holds these secrets
And yet it always knows
That if I reveal a bit too much
Into the fireplace it goes!

This is another poem that I started many years ago but never finished. I decided to finish it now, throwing in a few more life experiences that I've had since I started it. There is no question at all that I value education. I worked full-time while going to college, so I realize the sacrifice and commitment. But school or college is not the only path to learning. I know many people who never went to college and a few who never finished high school. As they would say, they went to the school of hard knocks, and some of them are the smartest people I know. They are honest and hard working and just all around decent people. The common sense and problem solving skills that they possess is amazing, yet they are looked down upon in some cases because they don't have that piece of paper with a few letters after their name.

I am not sure the Internet is helping either. We have more information available at our fingertips but I feel as if we are less informed than ever before. On top of that, our social skills are suffering, as so many people have their head buried in their devices. Look around at restaurants and see how many people are actually talking with one another. I am guilty of this also, as I often have my head buried in my phone or emails, and I spend more than eight hours of every day looking at a computer screen. I am glad that when I was in school, we did not have the internet. As handy as Google is, there was some satisfaction in spending long Saturdays at the library, pulling out the card catalog, thumbing through and writing down the location, finding that book on the shelf like a hidden treasure and bringing it and several others back to the table to compile research. As frustrating as microfiche was, again there was that satisfaction of homing in on the article you were searching for and hitting that print button. All of that is missing with today's technology. Imagine if there was a technology crash, which I suppose could happen at any time, and the world went off-line for a day or two, or even a week. Would you miss it, or would you feel some relief at being disconnected? Be honest.

I would never discourage anyone from going after their dream of getting an education, but I would also encourage them to sharpen their common sense and critical thinking skills, as well as their social skills, because once they walk off that graduation stage with that diploma in hand, the real world is there waiting, and it is not always kind.

LIFE LESSONS OUTSIDE THE CLASSROOM

College taught me many things
Like English, math, and science.
Meeting deadlines surely helped me
Nail down compliance.

Such as getting work turned in on time
Or studying for that test.
I never made the Dean's list
But I know I did my best.

College didn't prepare me
For matters of the heart,
Or how to pick myself back up
When life just fell apart.

Like when that romance took a turn
And I found out he had cheated;
College didn't teach me
That I'd often feel defeated.

In school I learned history
But not how to live today.
The present remains a mystery
As I learn to find my way.

College didn't prepare me
For matters that are real,
Like when my father passed away
And I didn't know how to deal.

Or when I held my beloved cat
As she whispered her last breath;
I learned about evolution
But not about life and death.

No college class has ever taught
My hurt soul how to cope,
Or how to lift my head each day
And face the world with hope.

Math and science are crucial
But the best lesson of all
Is to learn that we will walk again
Once we survive the fall.

For in each life are lessons
That we must learn on our own.
We realize an inner strength
When we walk the path alone.

Education has its value
I do believe that's true,
But when it comes to learning about life
The best teacher is you.

There are many things in life that I do not understand, and definitely on that list are dreams.

As Jerry Seinfeld would say, "What's the deal with dreams?!" What the heck happens when we fall asleep and where does our mind venture? How strange is it when you have a dream about someone you haven't seen or thought about in forever, and suddenly one night they happen to pop into your dream? Where does that come from? The spiritual side of me would like to think our souls exit our bodies each night and go on an adventure, but that seems a bit far-fetched. The more practical side of me thinks it is our brain defragmenting and downloading all of the information we absorb throughout the days and weeks and years in order to process it somehow and file it away into our memory banks. Dreams have been the topic of scientific, philosophical and religious interest throughout recorded history. So what are dreams? WebMD describes dreams as basically stories and images that our mind creates while we sleep. They can be vivid. They can make you feel happy, sad, or scared. And they may seem confusing or perfectly rational.

In most cases I find them to be confusing, if I remember them at all. One very vivid dream that I do remember is what some would describe as a visitation. I dreamt that my dad, who had already passed away, and I were driving around on a beautiful hilly countryside. We were in a yellow two-seater convertible and our hair was blowing around and we were having the best day together. When the dream came to an end and he told me he had to go, I was crying in my dream and reaching for him and begging him not to leave. When I woke up my face was wet with tears and my arm was in the air, reaching for something or someone. Was this a quick glance into the future, as the next poem will explain? This dream happened almost twenty-five years ago and I still remember it so clearly. It haunted me for days afterward.

It is always so strange to me when suddenly a person from my past or someone that played a very small role in my life appears in my dream. Usually that dream will stick with me for a while, wondering why and where it came from, and more importantly, did I reciprocate by popping into his or her dream? Another mystery I may never understand.

DREAMS

Have you ever been awoken
and jolted from your bed?
Someone you knew from long ago
Just popped into your head.

This person you just dreamt about,
You have not seen in years.
Suddenly your mind is racing,
Going through the gears.

They haven't played too big a role
In your life so far.
If you passed them on the street
You might not know who they are.

You shake your head and shrug it off;
A coincidence it would seem.
Yet you can't help but wonder
Why they appeared inside your dream.

The next day, as the day rolls on
Your mind keeps reverting
To this person who was in your dream;
Is it possible he was flirting?

You blush and shyly chalk it up
To dreams that make no sense.
But you wonder if he'll appear again
When tonight your dreams commence?

Whether he will emerge tonight
Is something no one knows.
You know you can't control
Who shows up while you doze.

But one thing that I wonder,
And something I do fear;
Whose dreams do I pop into at night,
And what am I doing while I'm there?!

The previous poem mentioned a dream I had years ago where my dad and I were taking a nice drive over the hillside in a yellow convertible. So, it was interesting when a few years later my mom ended up buying a yellow convertible, just like the one in my dream. My dad had been long passed at this point, and my mom was remarried to my stepdad, so my dad did not have any influence over that decision, at least not consciously. Was this dream a bit of foreshadowing? It must have all been just coincidental, as I had never told my mom about the dream. It was the early 2000s when my mom started to get the itch for a convertible. My sister and I were not on board with the idea and here's why: a few years earlier my stepdad had purchased a boat. I was thrilled as I love the hot weather and being out on a lake. There is nothing better in the summer! The plan was to take it out to the lake most weekends, but that did not pan out because we had the rainiest summer that year. We took it out a few times, and then the novelty wore off as each week we'd eagerly await the weekend weather forecast, and then our hopes would fall as once again it was predicted to be cool and rainy. The following summer, my boyfriend and I each bought the hundredth anniversary edition Harley- Davidson Motorcycles and mine was an 883 Sportster. Guess what? It was another wet and rainy summer. This ended up being a blessing though, because I could not seem to grasp keeping those two wheels upright, and after the third wipeout (this one more serious than the first two, but aside from my ego, thankfully no one was hurt), I decided this motorcycle hobby probably was not for me. Clearly, we did not have the weather Gods on our side when we invested in these summer toys.

As luck would have it, once the boat and the motorcycle were gone, we had a beautiful summer the following year, so when my mom announced that she wanted a convertible, we immediately thought she was going to jinx the weather for the rest of the season. One day they happened upon a little two-seater BMW Z3 Roadster, in a bright yellow and my mom was in love. Luckily the bad weather spell seemed to have moved on because we had some pretty nice summers from then on. They took this car to many places and had so much fun with it. An amusing story I remember is shortly after they got that little car, I was talking with my mom on the phone and she was complaining about how both she and my stepdad were putting on some weight, and she couldn't figure out why. I was asking her if they had changed their eating habits, or were sitting around too much, and she said no, nothing had changed. Then a few minutes later she said "Oh wait ... I know what it is. A couple of nights a week after dinner, we take the little car out for an evening ride ... to Oberweis!" I'm glad they figured that one out before they no longer fit in that little car!

Eventually my mom got sick, and this car was no longer safe or practical for her to drive, so it was going to be put up for sale. Memorial Day weekend was coming up and I asked if I could take the car home with me over the long weekend to see if I liked it. I took it out for a ride reluctantly, expecting to not like sitting so low in a car after having had a few Jeeps, but I surprised myself by falling in love with that car. I drove around that night with the sun setting and the wind in my hair, Robert Plant's song "Big Log" (very melodic) playing on the stereo, and I knew what my decision was going to be. I was not going to part with that car! I ended up buying it and each spring when I take it out for its first ride of the season the thrill is still there. As I drive around with the sun on my face and the music playing, probably louder than it should be, I know my angels on each shoulder are along for the ride.

Many people name their cars (remember *Christine?*), and I did the same by shortening it from "the little yellow car," to "Little Yellow," and eventually to L Y. Many songs have been written about cars and their owner's love for them, including "Red Barchetta" by Rush, "Little Red Corvette" by

Prince, "Mercedes Benz" by Janis Joplin, "Chevy Van" by Sammy Johns, "Greased Lightnin" from Grease, "80's Mercedes" by Maren Morris, and "Somethin"bout a truck" by Kip Moore, to name a few. It is no surprise that we feel a deep connection to these vehicles that give us so much pleasure and so many memories. I love going to car shows in the summer and seeing the pride people show in displaying their cars. And if you ask them a question about it, they will talk your ear off for hours! I have put L Y in a few car shows and I always love it when people come up and ask questions or tell me of their experiences with a similar car. Even when memories start to fade, seeing an old or familiar car can bring most people back to the days when it was love at first drive, or they have memories of their parents having owned that car or perhaps learning how to drive in one similar. Cars are such a big part of our history and for most of us they were our first taste of freedom. Almost everyone remembers their first car, and almost everyone remembers what they used to do in the back seats of those cars, but we won't get into that here!

This next poem is a tribute to this little car that brought my mom, and now me, so much joy. And unlike that motorcycle, I've been able to keep all four wheels firmly planted on the ground!

ODE TO THE LITTLE YELLOW CAR
(a.k.a. L Y)

When Mom wanted a convertible
We kids just rolled our eyes.
She found a little yellow one,
Imagine our surprise.

We thought it would just be a fad;
One season, it would be gone.
She had that car for thirteen years.
Once again, she proved us wrong.

My stepdad is quite a big guy
To fit a car so small,
But he drove that yellow car around
Without a care at all.

I saw them fly by one day
As I was pumping gas;
Their white hair flowing in the wind
As they quickly drove on past.

I could hear their music blasting out
From half a block away;
It was louder than it should be
As Frank Sinatra sang away.

Again I rolled my eyes at them,
But yet I had to grin.
They loved telling the stories
Of adventures they'd get in

They'd often take drives on summer nights
To the local ice-cream store.
A few weeks later, their pants too tight,
Those trips they were no more.

When Mom got sick, the car got parked
And was going to be sold.
"Let me take it for a ride," I said,
"Before I get too old."

To my surprise, I fell in love
And took it home with me.
I love the wind blowing my hair;
My music louder than should be.

Now I live for those summer nights
As I cruise from place to place.
I've got an angel on each shoulder,
And a smile upon my face.

In my previous book, I included a poem I wrote several years ago called "Today I Give My Love." That poem became my sister and brother-in-law's wedding invitation. It was thrilling to see my words in print and being mailed out to so many people as a way to kick off their marriage.

This next poem was the runner-up. I am not sure why we chose the one that we did and all these years later it doesn't really matter. As long as the result was a happy ending, and since the happy couple is close to celebrating their thirtieth wedding anniversary, I'd say it was a success!

LIFE'S REWARD

Dear Lord, you must have heard my prayers
For you have given me
A love so true it will outshine
The sun, the stars, the sea.

Today we celebrate this love.
I thank you so, Dear Lord.
For love, when it is truly right
Is life's finest reward.

From this day forward I shall spend
A lifetime loving my best friend.

Remember when you were a little kid and you would chant "Sticks and stones may break my bones, but words will never harm me"? Well guess what? It's not true. Words can and do harm, and sometimes they cause irrevocable damage. Have you ever had a moment where you said something, maybe directly to someone or under your breath, and instantly wished you could take it back? It is a helpless feeling when you realize there is nothing you can do, as your words float around in the atmosphere like little missiles targeting someone you care about. This happened to me recently, and resulted in this next poem. Similar to the woman in the earlier poem, "Reflections of the Day", I too had let little things creep up on me and steal my joy and my kindness, and this frustration grew inside of me until it came out in an aggressive and hostile way. Fortunately, unlike the woman in the poem, I did not witness a car crash to jolt me out of my own head, but the disappointment I saw on this person's face was enough of a wake-up call. Anger can be a slippery slope, and once you start the descent downhill it is hard to regain your footing.

Hopefully, when you go through these hard times with someone and get to the other side, you come out stronger. Sometimes the words lead to deeper discussion to get to the root of the anger or frustration and to try to understand what prompted them to be spoken in the first place. In the end it can lead to a stronger bond between the two of you, but that is not always the case. Sometimes things cannot be worked out, as anger and resentment sets in for the person who was targeted, and guilt and regret for the person who spoke the words. All involved may carry these words around with them for a long time. I wrote about this previously; how memories can be heavy and a burden. In order to unleash this burden, sometimes all we can do is go to the person, hat in hand, and offer our most humble and sincere apology and hope that it will be accepted. It may not be. We cannot control how someone will respond. All we can do is control our own actions, and sometimes that involves eating a little crow and admitting that we were wrong, and hoping for the best possible outcome so that we can move forward in peace.

HUMBLE PIE

I'd like to send a sappy card
As a way to make amends.
And to let you know, deep in my heart,
I'm so grateful that we're friends.

How lucky I am that you are such
A big part of my world.
I'm sorry for the words I used
When my thoughts became unfurled.

I'd love to travel back in time,
Or click Edit Undo.
I wish I could backspace, erase,
Those things I said to you.

I knew that I had gone too far
As my words began to fumble.
I could see when they sunk in for you,
And your face started to crumble.

In that moment, guilt and fear
Took place inside my soul,
As I pictured my life without you there
And I felt an endless hole.

We always hurt the ones we love;
Isn't that what they say?
But how much can we push and push,
Before we push away?

We always hurt the ones we love;
Again that's how it goes.
Yet still they seem to find the will
To remain as friends, not foes.

Do we deserve this second chance?
At times I'm not so sure.
There has to be a limit as to
How much they endure.

In moments of such tension
We feel that we are doomed,
As remorse rushes to the scene
To bandage up the wound.

But the heart forgives, when sometimes it shouldn't
And things can be rectified;
As healing starts, and hugs take place,
And relief flows through inside.

A lesson learned; words can hurt,
And actions can destroy.
Feelings sometimes don't bounce back,
And emotions are not a toy.

Sticks and stones may break the bones,
But words, they too can break;
And being careless with our words
Can lead to this mistake.

I am grateful for forgiveness
In ways I can't define.
I realize I hurt you –
And I know I crossed a line.

I'll treasure that forgiveness
Until the day I die.
I make a promise to not repeat,
As I digest my humble pie.

In the poem about the little yellow convertible, I mentioned that when I ride around in that car, I have an angel on each shoulder, referencing my mom and dad, who have both passed. A few days ago while listening to a podcast, the host mentioned how she had purchased something that she should not have bought, and said the devil on her shoulder had won out with that purchase. That inspired me to entertain this concept of the angel or devil on our shoulder, and the whisperings of each that we listen to at different times. I am sure we have all seen cartoon depictions of someone struggling with a decision and the angel with the halo is on one side and the devil with his pitchfork is on the other and the person is looking back and forth trying to decide which voice to listen to. I have certainly allowed the devil on my own shoulder to win out when I have also purchased things I probably shouldn't have, or engaged in reckless behavior when I knew better.

I mentioned when I was discussing "The Storm Inside" how we are all fighting our own internal battles and we do not know what other people are dealing with, so a little kindness goes a long way. However, as I also admitted, I have my own struggles with being kind on occasion, so at those moments I know that pesky devil on my shoulder is winning out. But alas, I always seem to shake it off and realize when I have been unkind or could have made a better decision, and I know the angel on my other shoulder has stepped forward to guide me in the other direction. Oftentimes it comes down to a battle between right and wrong, good and bad, kind and cruel. Usually for me I have found common ground somewhere in the middle. I am never going to be a perfect human, none of us are, and there are always things that I will look back upon and realize I could have done better. I will never have an entirely sunny disposition all the time. There will be some bad moods that creep in even though life is very good and I am grateful for all of the blessings that have come my way. In my heart I know that I am a good person at the core and even though that devil does win out sometimes and the negativity creeps in, I can usually kick it to the curb pretty quickly.

In this poem you can really hear the internal struggle that the person is going through as he or she tries to shake off the dark mood. We all go through this when we want something we know we shouldn't have or should not do and we try to justify the decision in any way we can. Right or wrong we need to be prepared to live with the consequences of that decision. In moments of struggle, that is when we have to decide which voice we will embrace, and which voice we will ignore.

Have you ever heard the Native American parable of the story of the two wolves? In this story an older Cherokee Indian is teaching his grandson about life and the struggles within. He explains that a fight is going on inside of him, and the fight is between two wolves. One of the wolves is evil; full of anger, resentment, greed, among many other ugly characteristics. The other wolf is good; full of peace, love, hope, joy, compassion, humility, and the list of positive attributes goes on and on. The elder Cherokee explains to the boy that this same fight is going on within every person. After giving it some thought, the boy asks which wolf will win. The Cherokee responded simply, "The one you feed."

THE DEVIL ON MY SHOULDER

All the affirmations say
To wake up with gratitude.
I try my best, but there are days
I am just not in the mood.

For reasons that I cannot explain
My temper just feels sour.
But to change my frame of mind today
Seems far outside my power.

I rather enjoy this feeling
Of being irritable and weary.
The weather seems to match my mood;
It is overcast and dreary.

I know I should erase this mood
But I fear it will remain.
The world grips my darkness
As the clouds release the rain.

Do I give in to the negative
And let it win this round?
Or do I fight with all my might
To turn bad thoughts around?

I hope that I am wrong
And I hope it goes away,
But I think the devil on my shoulder
Will win the fight today.

But the angel on my other shoulder
Makes her presence known
As she steps forth to let the devil
Know he's not alone.

And it begins, a struggle,
As the angel takes a chance
To try to turn my gloom around
As they begin a dance.

Waiting to see which side I'll pick;
Which side will I choose?
Will I let my angel overtake
And chase away the blues?

Or will I let the devil win
As I fight to pick a side;
Determining what my soul needs,
And what each one can provide?

The devil on my one shoulder
Wants me to be hateful,
While the angel on my other side
Persuades me to be grateful.

I can't linger in this foul mood
So I have to make a choice.
Which one can sooth my soul
With the more appealing voice?

It is hard to fully pick a side
When the world has so much strife.
But who wants to walk around all day
Mad at the world and at life?

No one wants to stay here
Fighting this internal war,
As I lean toward the bright side
And the darkness I ignore.

But then, I rather like the dark
As I try to plead my case.
But the bright side is more alluring
As the voice I *should* embrace.

There's a lot in the world to fret about,
And the world can be unkind.
But knowing that we can change our thoughts
Can bring some piece of mind.

A positive mind is something that
We all can take control.
Embracing the hopeful thoughts inside
Can help to sooth our soul.

But the darkness doesn't quite disappear
Although we wish it could.
In this race that we call human
There is bad among the good.

Here I am, in the middle of both
So I will pick a middle ground.
I'll choose a little of each one
As my bitterness turns around.

I feel a little lighter
As the dark starts to ascend.
I pull myself together
And the bad mood starts to mend.

I smile a bit, feeling relief
As I kick away the gray.
Sorry, devil on my shoulder …
Today is not your day.

When I was growing up my dad typically worked half a day every Saturday, so our job as kids was to have the house clean when he walked through the door around 1:00 p.m. I suppose the structure was a good thing and kids do need that, but this is one of those nagging habits that I brought with me into adulthood. Don't get me wrong, having a clean house or doing chores is not a bad thing, except when it interferes with life. In the past if someone would invite me to something on a Saturday, I would immediately feel that anxiety kick in as if to say "what about the housework?" I wish I could rid myself of the need to always put that first, but it is a hard habit to break after having it ingrained from childhood. I have gotten better though. A few years ago I had surgery and could not clean or vacuum for several weeks. Guess what happened? Nothing! Well, aside from the house getting very dusty and dirty, the world did not end! I often refer back to that time when life gets crazy and the house gets a little out of sorts. I tell myself that it is OK and that living life is so much more important than getting chores done. After all, who ever said at the end of their life "Boy, I am really proud of my clean house"?

Now, as I am getting older and everyone is so busy or even moving away as we get closer to retirement, I am realizing more and more the value in spending time with those people whom we cherish, especially as I have already lost people in my life. My sister has a plaque with a poem on it hanging on her wall that she got when my niece was born, and it is written from the viewpoint of a young mother. The ending of the poem talks about how all the unimportant stuff can wait because this young mother is rocking her baby, and babies don't keep. I always loved that poem. I have learned that people don't keep either. We always think there is tomorrow, or next week, or next year, but the truth is, sometimes there is not.

This next poem was written after I had met a dear friend for lunch on a weekend. It was one of those situations where we finally made the time after saying "We need to get together" one too many times. We sat down at 2:00 p.m. and talked and laughed and got caught up. At one point, a friend of my friend saw us through the window and came in to have a drink with us, which was such an unexpected pleasure. I thought it was about 5:00 p.m. when I looked at my watch and saw that it was 7:20! We had been there for over five hours! No wonder our rumps were sore. When I got home about 8:00 p.m., I looked around at all the stuff that did not get done that weekend and immediately felt a pang of guilt. But I quickly shrugged it off as I would not have changed a thing about spending the afternoon with my friend. I am getting better at letting the small stuff go and embracing the important moments in life, because like those babies, these opportunities to see loved ones don't keep either.

TIME SPENT WITH FRIENDS

I met a friend for lunch today,
We found the time at last.
We talked and laughed and got caught up,
The hours flew on past.

We sat for hours on those same seats;
Our bottoms started aching!
We reminisced about old times
And the memories we were making.

When I got home I realized
How much did not get done.
The laundry did not wash itself
While I was out having fun.

The dishwasher still sat quite full.
There are no clean coffee mugs.
The floor is in need of sweeping
And there's cat hair on the rugs.

Something is rotting in the fridge
As I quickly close the door.
My side eye catches dust bunnies
scampering across the floor.

The bathtub needs a scrubbing
And there are streaks across the mirror.
I feel a flash of guilt inside;
I should've stayed right here.

But life is short, and friends are few,
And fewer every year,
As life takes us in separate ways
From those we hold so dear.

That to-do list will still be there,
And the chores may never end.
But what can be so fleeting
Is the time we spend with friends.

So do not pause or vacillate
When a friend sends an invitation.
The chance to see those dear to you
Should come without hesitation.

The errands will be waiting
And the world, it won't end
But your soul will be smiling
Because you hugged your friend.

I smile as I recall the laughs
And the great wine that we tasted.
I've learned that time spent with friends
Is never time that's wasted.

Every year my friends and I get together for our annual summer outing. It is an entire day, starting with breakfast, then onto the adventure that one of us planned, and then back to my friend's house in the early afternoon for appetizers and drinks followed by dinner. It is a fun day and one that I look forward to every year. This year though, I was really struggling with a relationship issue, so I wasn't feeling my usual jovial self. However, I did not want to bring the mood of the day down, so I tucked the sadness down deep and put on a happy face and went about the day. It helped to take my mind off everything. Later that night after dinner, I found out that one of my friends was also dealing with a personal issue, but she too had tucked it away for the day but finally ended up talking about it at the end of the night, which resulted in tears. As I drove home a while later, I started thinking about how each of us was in pain, and even while spending the day together we had no idea what the other was struggling with. I discussed this earlier in my poem "The Storm Inside," about how everyone is dealing with some kind of issue, and some people show it all over their face, while most of us tuck it away and go about the day as if nothing is amiss. Neither way is right or wrong in my opinion. We each just have different ways of dealing with discomfort and choosing what we will share with the world, or each other.

So, if we are all comrades in suffering, shouldn't we be banding together and rooting for the same team, cheering each other on toward peace and happiness? Instead for the most part, as a society we remain so divided. This is not always the case, as I have seen many people come together during times of tragedy by starting GoFundMe pages, or various other fundraisers to help families impacted by misfortune. Just recently, areas close to my town were impacted by tornadoes and neighbors came out in droves to help each other, and it was wonderful to see good coming from bad. But in many instances, pain creates gaps and distances as many people sink into themselves like a turtle into its shell when danger is near. I feel like we still focus so much on our differences, rather than our similarities. There could be two people fighting the same illness, sitting in a doctor's waiting room, seeking the same treatment. If there is a television on and it happens to be on a political channel, if these two people sitting in this same room are on opposite sides, those opposing views will become their focus, not the illness they share. I think that is just human nature. If ten people say nice things about a person, but one person says something negative or unkind, what will be stuck inside the person's head? I am guessing it will be the off-putting comment, as the negative always seems to win out. I am not sure why we embrace the negative and let it consume the good and positive things all around us. Like that wolf in the Indian parable, we continue to feed it and it continues to grow. We should not give it that power.

What if we were all just a little more patient with each other, and extended that grace and kindness as I mentioned before? What if we tried to build bridges rather than watching them burn all around us?

As a wise man named John Lennon once said "Imagine ..."

EVERY DAY

Every day a new heart breaks.
Somebody sheds a tear.
Someone looks down the barrel of a gun
And contemplates why they're here.

Every day someone fights to survive
As someone loses the fight to live.
Every day someone just takes and takes,
While others try so hard to give.

Millions of people hurt every day
As they try to hold onto their pride.
Millions of tears fall every day
As someone quietly dies inside.

Every day someone struggles with life.
No one, it seems, is immune.
Some people tuck the pain deep down inside
While others display in full bloom.

Every day millions of people pray
For the solace that they seek.
With so many people in such desperation,
Is our own pain all that unique?

> If we are all comrades in pain
> With the demons that live inside us,
> Shouldn't we all band together as one?
> Instead we let difference divide us.
>
> Millions of people hurt every day
> In ways they cannot define.
> Millions of tears fall every day.
> Today those tears are mine.
>
> I wonder if I am selfish,
> Focusing on my own grief;
> But I look around at the world at large,
> And pray that we *all* find relief.

A previous poem talks about how while I was having lunch with my friend, a friend of hers saw us through the window and stopped in to have a drink with us. I had never met this woman but I immediately liked her laid back style, and kindness just radiated out of her. She had such a great energy. As we were talking about all kinds of things, she was explaining her current living situation, which was in a bit of a transition. She was trying to figure out her next move, which would need to happen within the next few months. As she was weighing all the different options, she stopped herself and took a breath and said, "Maybe I should just let life unfold." I immediately said cheers to that, as we toasted, but aside from that, I just loved that line and that attitude, so I immediately filed it away for future reference.

Many times in life we stress ourselves out so much worrying about "what if" or things outside of our control. We want structure and we try to plan for every eventuality. When things do not go the way we planned, we are disappointed or thrown off course, or anxiety overtakes us as we try to figure out Plan B. But this takes some of the spontaneity and fun out of life. Shouldn't part of life be a mystery? Isn't part of the gift of life wondering what is inside the package? If we had all the answers or had carefully planned every detail, life would possibly run a little smoother, but then again, maybe not. Life has a funny way of showing us who is boss, and usually it is not us.

Remember the movie *Groundhog Day* with Bill Murray? Every day his character would awaken to the same day over and over again. At first he used it to his advantage, knowing everything that was going to happen that day and being able to plan for it. But as each day repeated itself, he grew more and more frustrated for that very same reason! Every day was the same and it was all planned out and he knew what to expect. His life had lost that spontaneity and impulsiveness. That starts to happen to a lot of us. Imagine if you had the opportunity to see your life unfold in a crystal ball and you knew what to expect throughout the years. Would you want to know? On the one hand, you could plan for it and be ready and this might help you to feel more in control of things. But then, on the other hand, there would be no surprises. Life is supposed to be a journey, and part of every journey is bumps along the way. It is not only the bumps that shape us and our character, it is how we respond to those bumps and how we allow the road that we're traveling to shift a little under our feet as we find new ground. So we should embrace that bumpy road, with all its twists and turns, hold on tight, and let life unfold.

LET LIFE UNFOLD

From the time that we are little tots
We learn the golden rule.
Conformity and routine
Were other things we learned in school.

As we grow up and start to form
A life to call our own
The structure and the rules we learned
Stick with us to the bone.

We lose some of the playfulness
And spontaneity.
We start to live by calendars
That tell us where to be.

Maybe we should take a break
From doing what we're told.
Grab back some impulsiveness
And just let life unfold.

Sometimes we want to write our life
Right down to the last minute.
We want to dictate all the plans
And all the people in it.

And then when things don't work out
We shrug and wonder why.
We often feel like giving up;
Why should we even try?

So many things in life
Are outside of our hands.
If you ever want to hear God laugh
Just tell him of your plans.

We don't know what the future holds
So it does not pay to worry.
Life will pass on its own time;
Don't be in such a hurry.

We want to quickly check things off,
And move on down the list.
While we're busy crossing off things we did
There is so much we just missed.

So maybe we should relax those reins,
Be a bit more carefree.
I hear that there's a plan for us,
And what will be, will be.

We never know what life has in store
When we step out of the mold.
So take a breath, and hold on tight,
And just let life unfold!

This poem does not need much explanation behind the motivation, and I put it near the end on purpose as a reminder to not only be kind to each other, but also to ourselves. I am sure I wrote it one day when I was feeling especially haggard, at the end of a busy weekend where I finally sat down and then realized it was time to go to bed because Monday morning would be knocking soon. How often do we do that? We spend so much of our time going through the motions of getting things done; dealing with work, kids, after school activities, spouses, social invitations, etc. These are not bad things and there is nothing wrong with devoting time to them, as long as it is where you want to be placing your time and effort. If your time is taken up doing things that you do not want to be doing, such as going to a job that you hate or attending social events when you would rather be at home snuggled up on the couch, that is when things start to chip away at us. Once we start allowing ourselves to be chipped away, we start to become weaker and less effective at everything. A weaker person is more vulnerable to attack, and that is when stress starts to manifest itself inside of us in harmful ways. So what is our best defense? We need to take stock of the things in life that are really important to us and decide where we want to spend our time. We cannot give away so much of ourselves that we start to become bitter or angry toward life, or the important people in our lives. If pieces of us are missing or we are spread too thin, it is hard to be kind to others as we get into a self protective and defensive mode. The more of ourselves that we hold onto, the more we have to give to others. It is easier to be happier, and kinder, when we are in one whole piece and not scattered all over. So share yourself with others, but don't lose yourself in the process.

PIECES OF US

We all give so much of our time
To others every day.
What pieces do we keep for ourselves?
What do we take away?

What pieces of us do we keep
And what do we hold dear?
Where do we draw the line and say,
"I have no more to spare"?

We spend so much time at work each week
But if we passed away,
Our family would grieve forever.
Our boss would replace us the next day.

We stress over work deadlines
That interfere with health.
We sacrifice our own good will
Just to increase our wealth.

What good is it to have that house
With all that extra space?
We could enjoy the benefits
If we'd just slow our pace.

We say yes to invites
When we really should say no.
We dread it until the time comes near
But yet we always go.

We spend our weekends doing chores
Instead of recreation.
It's taking pieces of our lives
But we don't see the degradation.

And then suddenly the time is gone
As we deal with the strife.
We wonder where the pieces went
In the puzzle of our life.

We try to hold on a little more
As we pine for one more day.
But there is nothing left of us anymore;
We gave it all away.

A wise man by the name of Forrest Gump once said, "Life is like a box of chocolates. You never know what you're gonna get." I think that quote meant that life is full of surprises and uncertainties, and you just have to take a bite and hope for the best. I am going to take it in a different direction and say that sometimes life is so crazy and busy, that by the time you get around to enjoying it you'll find that everyone else has rummaged through before you and taken all the best pieces, leaving only the hollow and bitter pieces behind. I hope that as you go through your life, you are taking care and not spreading yourself too thin. I hope that you are sharing parts of yourself with others, as that is what life's all about, but I also hope that you are keeping some of the best pieces of yourself for yourself!

K.A. Bloch

SCATTER SEEDS OF KINDNESS

Wherever you may go.
You never know what may take root
Or what magic they might grow.
Walk through a field of flowers
And scatter them with a shake.
You never know whose life you'll touch
By the seeds left in your wake.

ACKNOWLEDGMENTS

To all the supporters of my first book who asked that question "When is the next book coming out?" You scattered a seed that was planted within my heart and that seed grew into this book. So I thank you for the encouragement!

I also want to thank you greatly for spending your time with me reading this book. Once again, I hope you find something that touched your soul!

To my sister Sue who has become my biggest promoter, telling everyone wherever she goes about my book. Thank you!

As always, to my wonderful friends and family who always have my back! Love to you all!

And last (but not least!) I want to thank God. I don't do that enough ... say thank you for all the blessings in my life. Recently I purchased a plaque that says, *"God put that dream in your heart for a reason."* I hung it above my desk, and I look at it often, especially when I am in need of motivation. I am not sure if this book is the dream that the plaque was referring to, and I am not sure of the reason, but if just one person finds some hope or inspiration, then that is reason enough for me.

ABOUT THE AUTHOR

Kristin first began rhyming words together at a very young age. Soon these words expanded into poems and stories that enchanted family and friends. A compilation of those writings was recently released in her first book, *Walk Through a Field of Flowers*. Kristin works full-time and has earned a MBA degree from the University of Phoenix. Kristin is also a certified personal trainer and certified Pilates instructor, teaching several classes each week. This is her second book.

www.ingramcontent.com/pod-product-compliance
Lightning Source LLC
LaVergne TN
LVHW011855060526
838200LV00054B/4337